don't look back

MOIRA ALEXANDER

Ark House Press
arkhousepress.com

Some names and identifying details have been changed to protect the privacy of individuals.

Cataloguing in Publication Data:
Title: Don't Look Back
ISBN: 978-1-7641362-3-5 (pbk)
Subjects: REL012170 RELIGION / Christian Living / Personal Memoirs; REL012040 RELIGION / Christian Living / Inspirational;

Design by initiateagency.com

With dear thanks to my lovely friend Phyllis

Introduction

This is my story of hope and a future to show you how amazing Jesus is. I am nobody special. However, I have been told to write down my experiences to share with you. Life is not easy, but I have found that relying on Him makes it possible. There are good days and bad days. Luckily for us, Jesus comes with us through each. I was scared and did not believe that I should have any help getting out of the situation that I had found myself in. It has been a mixed experience, wondering what lay ahead some days. I could not imagine how I would have gotten through the last 20 years if I did not have Jesus to rely on. I chat with Him throughout each day.

Please be encouraged by this story of mine. It was hard, but most of the time I had the peace of God, except when I stepped away (Jesus never did). Sometimes when all is looking lost, you have to stop and take stock of the blessings that are around you. (There will be one somewhere).

I have had a few moments along the way, but I am glad that I took each step of faith and walked along the path with Jesus. I can walk and not grow weary or faint. I am the quirkiest Christian that I know. I am really quite silly and I often have a joke with Jesus. I am sure he thinks, 'Oh no. What now?' I always take him everywhere I go and sometimes I am sure He really doesn't want to go where I have gone. Anyway, luckily Jesus loves me and is happy to take me by the hand and walk along together.

I hope you appreciate reading about my strange and wonderful journey and maybe take some inspiration from it.

ENJOY!

Wed 13th September 2023

Up Early.

Simon has gone to work at 5.45am as usual.

Simon is my partner of 20 years. 20 long, horrific years of emotional domestic violence.

Suitcases out and start bundling books and souvenirs in. Make a cup of tea (always need a tea when everything is going badly) and put washing on. Jemma on the phone (all clear). She is on truck duty.

Jesus has arranged a truck (not a van that I booked). Must have shook his head and said, 'No. What exactly are you fitting in that?'

Yes, I believe in Jesus. I have an amazing relationship with him, but I haven't been to church in the last 20 years. I am currently living in captivity. Also in sin (I am aware). Not married and have three children: Samantha, Nick and Melissa. However, Jesus loves me and is getting me back on track.

Everybody on deck, including Nick, who doesn't seem too happy to be leaving actually. Not really bringing much, so I have had to add to his collection.

Nick is our son, 18 years old, and as it turns out does not understand why I am leaving his 'Wonderful Dad'. I told all three of them, please stay if you want to. I meant it. After all, he is their father. Of course, this did not apply to Samantha, who he had taken a dislike to for no apparent reason.

Very hard to decide what to grab and what to leave. Birds are going to Jemma's in Nick's car. We can't have them in a rental.

This all seems quite surreal. No time to panic or stress, which is lucky, I guess. So much going on right now. Mum is dying in hospital. Serena (my boss) is selling her company, where I have worked for the last 20 years, since kids were babies. She is panicking that Simon will turn up tomorrow when the new owner is coming for an inspection. She wants me to cancel this move today (I don't think so!).

Have arranged power and gas on at the new place for some time today. Have been gradually taking some things over that wouldn't be missed for last two weeks. Have had a shed full at Serena's; things I have been collecting for last 20 years in readiness for this very day. Hasn't been nice here since Samantha was born, most of the time.

Met Simon after Patrick. Patrick and I married in the church 10 years prior. Patrick was gay. Trying hard not to be gay, but as I say it would be like me trying really, really hard to BE gay. Not gonna work!!'

So along comes a guy who is the opposite of gay. Homophobic actually. So charming and trying so very hard to please me with intervals of making me feel like I am not worthy of being with him.

- I have no money.
- I am from a failed marriage

Sometimes he would cancel a date last minute just to be cruel and to keep me keen, I guess. Anyway as usual with me, I was so grateful just to have someone interested in this useless, old, ugly person, that I enjoyed the good times with him.

Eventually he decided that he wanted a relationship after I said that I was moving on. He begged me to come back, promising everything. Then we got pregnant with Samantha.

I moved in and immediately it was hell. We had a ritual where he would up and leave every morning to go to his mum who would drop everything, while he sat and she served him food.

Then he would come back. He didn't go to talk to her, just purely to eat and then leave. I was excited to collect baby things, but I got screamed at because they weren't what he wanted. Then one night he woke me up at midnight to cook him food because he was hungry and needed to be served. I was exhausted as I was pregnant and working full time. I couldn't believe he was so selfish. I cried all the time, but pretended it was OK and tried my hardest to cook, clean, work and go to his parent's house with a smile on my face, even though I knew they hated me and wished I was from their culture and an arranged marriage.

Simon was always complaining that I was sick, and I must admit I was. However, I still did absolutely everything; it was just ten times harder than normal. Strangely, since moving, I haven't been sick. Maybe it was the stress or the mould that seemed to be all over that cold, dark house, even though I was constantly trying to remove it and always being told it was my fault it was there as I didn't clean enough.

Thank goodness for Jemma. Haven't spoken to her for at least five years and at the first sign of trouble, there she is. Such a lot of stuff to move. So busy and then another phone call from the hospital. Mum is very unwell. Is it OK to up her morphine and take her off breathing machine and just onto oxygen?

Yes, of course. Nurse puts us on speaker while we are in the kitchen. Myself, Jemma and Melissa. I say we love her so much and we are currently in the middle of moving, with Jemma helping with the truck. Nurse says Mum is nodding and smiling. I am so upset, but also so stressed about Simon and so very busy.

Arranged the rental from a weekend away recently in August. Had a meltdown – yes, could no longer cope with everything. Everything being Mum – sick, Serena – selling, so much work to do at home and Simon never happy with me. So Melissa at camp and no reason why I shouldn't go and chill for a few days, or so I thought. Simon had other ideas. Not happy again. Wonders why I am having a meltdown? He is going to drive me to hospital to be admitted to a mental institution, as I have obviously got mental health issues if I can't cope with my life.

Dinners have been cooked and frozen for him. Mum has been taken to her hospital appointments and no need to take Melissa to school. However, he was so angry that I cancelled the trip. Then he said, 'Oh you should have gone'. So OK, I rang back and re-booked. Was so, so very angry now. Oh well, still going.

Wednesday morning took Melissa to school camp bus and started 4 hour drive. Initially panicking then as I got further away – feeling better and better and so free and relaxed. Obviously right thing to do. Rang Mum. She is good and glad I am going away.

Rang Simon – he is furious. Glad I am not there. Better without me. I should move out permanently. Again!!! Keeps telling me this. Ok now I am getting sick of being told to leave. I feel abandoned and totally alone. I have nowhere to go. So I ring Brett, who is a friend of a friend. Get your Real Estate friend on the job. I am leaving. I never want to feel completely at a loss ever again. So we start the ball rolling. Find a place you are interested in. Find a few on the website and have to fill in rental application. This is very scary.

Off to day spa in the morning. All by myself. A bit scary but oh well – suck it up! Ended up being amazing. So relaxing. Yoga in the pool was so amazing overlooking the most beautiful view. So glad I came. Eventually have to go back.

As I was leaving, I watched a Christian TV show first that said, 'Sometimes you just have to stand down here on Earth and yell up to Heaven – Help, Help, Help!!' which is what I did. In the morning I turned on the TV and the Christian show was finishing. Oh no, I thought I missed it. The man was finishing up and he said, 'Goodbye everyone and remember, Jesus is Lord!!' Then it ended. Jesus said that's all I wanted you to hear. That's all you need to know. I am Lord!!

Time is ticking during moving day. Samantha is back from work so we have to go see Grandma. I leave Jemma and Melissa unpacking truck. Apparently they don't need me anyways. I really did try to help. Not good at manual stuff, I know. Off to hospital. Mum in Palliative Care room now. It is not good, I know. She is so, so bad. She is trying to be OK but she just isn't. I tell her we are moving in now. She can't speak. She smiles and thumbs up. We have to leave as she is so, so tired. Samantha is so distraught. She can barely stand up. She cannot stop crying. We hug. It is awful. Staff are concerned. One says it is very confronting what we are dealing with. They don't know the half of it. We leave. It's the last time we see her. I tell her I will come back to see her in the morning.

Back to new place via police station. Simon will find out soon. It will not be good. Policeman is worried for our safety. We don't look OK. I explain we have just come from hospital, which is why we don't look OK. I haven't eaten for a few days now. Losing lots of weight, which is good, but also bad. Can't imagine eating. Can't swallow. Rang Simon. He is not happy – What have I done?

Everyone is here. We have single mattresses on the floors. I am in the downstairs bedroom. I wake up at 3am. I feel very strange. In a new place. Simon is upset. Mum is in hospital. Kids are in new situation. Phone rings 4.30am. Mum is gone!!! Mum is gone!!! Oh my goodness. I can't cope or go on. Everything has changed. How am I supposed to continue on? I do not know. I seriously do not know!! I am crying hysterically. Ok must be time for a cup of tea. Head upstairs and put kettle on, where my crying has woken up Melissa.

Mum started going downhill in July 2023. She wasn't hungry. She had still been driving by herself up until then.

Thursday 13th July – Unwell at shopping and into hospital for a few days.

Thursday 27th July – To the doctor together.

Tuesday 8th August – To Neurologist.

Thursday 17th August – Numb leg. To hospital one day only.

Thursday 24th August – Mum Telehealth apointment. Picked up shower chair.

Monday 4th September – Rang doctor – Mum to hospital for chest x-ray (coughing).

Thursday 14th September – Mum dead!

Thursday 14th September

Melissa is going to school today. Can you believe yesterday she packed and unpacked a truck. Moved out of the only house she has ever known and in the middle of everything managed to locate some of her clothes, get dressed up, walked to a job interview (which she got). Then came back, had minimal sleep, woke up, found out grandma was dead and got ready and is going to school. As you would! She is only 16.

Nick is also going to Uni.

Samantha is at a friend's house. I have to ring her to tell her about Mum. Of course she is very upset. She knew when she saw her yesterday she said, which is why she was so overwhelmingly upset at the hospital. Also have to ring Rodney (brother) as he doesn't know yet either.

As usual I will be organising everything. Not sure why – just happens. No one else will be doing it I suppose. So funeral place and relatives to be contacted.

Going to go to church on Sunday. Big sign down the road within walking distance. Has been a long time since being to church. I have been in captivity by myself but with Jesus all the way. The only reason I am out and safe now is because of a Godly miracle. After my trip away, when I got back, I was in trouble from Simon. Things were OK but I knew he was angry again that I had gone. At night I was Googling Bible verses and quotes. I found a website outlining 3 things telling you to move on from a relationship:

1. If you read the Word and realise this person is not producing the fruits of the spirit outlined in Galatians 5:22-23;
2. You pray and feel like Holy Spirit is telling you to let this relationship go;
3. You look at the history of dysfunction in this relationship that has happened in real life.

If all 3 of these are present you can be confident you have a sign from God. God says, *"Be ye not unequally yoked together with unbelievers."* 2 Corinthians 6:14

"Flee fornication." 1 Corinthians 6:18.
"Flee also youthful lusts." 2 Timothy 2:22

So we should walk away in the other direction and DON'T LOOK BACK.

I kept feeling to go. Leave. Trust in God and very importantly **do not look back** (like Lot's wife). However I did look back and this made my decision and new life more difficult than it should have been.

Simon and I spoke after I left. He kept ringing me. He didn't understand why I left. He didn't know I was unhappy. I should come back immediately. I was stressing out the kids. Are we going to waste the last 20 years? We should have dinner and discuss. He didn't mean everything he said over the last 20 years. He was just joking. Let's remember a few things that he was joking about shall we?

- Apparently everybody else has had the best of me. He should have listened to his mother and never been with me.
- Do not put rubbish in our bin. Rubbish must be sorted all throughout the house in different rooms.
- Do not wear shoes or slippers on certain parts of floors. Sometimes shoes, sometimes slippers, sometimes socks. Never, ever bare feet (which I missed).

- Must religiously go grocery shopping at exactly the same time every week. Must not speak. People must not get in the way or will be rammed with trolley.
- I am a lazy (insert expletive) who is always sick.
- I should not be working. I should clean the house. (Wouldn't speak to me when I worked an extra shift once).
- Hated anything I bought or organised. Bought a small gift for him that I thought he might like. He was so angry – Why? Why? How much did that cost?
- I made a cake and bought wine for Father's Day. Shouldn't have done that - He doesn't like Father's Day.
- Was so sick with flu once. Unable to walk. Had to crawl to kitchen to cook and use the vegetables he had bought for dinner.
- Fell off bike and hurt my arm. He was so angry that bike was not fixable. Had me in tears for days. Had to buy a new bike and pretend they gave it to me for free. The man at the bike shop gave it to me at a cheaper price as I was so distraught.
- Abused a customer service man so much, I had to pay an extra month he believed he should not have to pay, to stop any more abusive phone calls to them.
- Screamed when I took toilet paper roll from the wrong side of his toilet roll stack. "Don't I f#@*ing know?"

Of course the worst behaviour was towards Samantha though.

Initially kicked her out in the street because she wouldn't cook for him. I was at work. Melissa rang me somehow and said "Mummy Samantha gone." I drove around until I found her alone walking to my workplace and crying. He was not fussed or worried at all.

Second time he kick her out was later. He had been talking about how much he hated her (I don't know why as she hadn't done anything other than say no to his angry demands such as cooking, sorting rubbish, shoes on carpet, etc.). He approached her when she was arriving home from work one day. "Right" He said "So you can hand over your keys – you're out!!" I was devastated. I did not know what to do.

I started looking for rentals at this stage. I think he knew, so he backed down and said she could "stay to keep you happy." But he didn't want her there. Then again in August 2022 he went ballistic at her for not wearing slippers and screamed right in her face while I was there to get the f out. That was when I found a rental but backed out at the last minute as I was terrified of the unknown.

Sometimes I wonder if I have made a big mistake and I should go back. Panic sets in. How will I afford things? What will become of me and our family in the future? Then I need to just pray and ask for "the peace that transcends all understanding." I also have to "not look back". Looking back I have realised is not good for me to continue moving forward. It makes me think that all was not so bad. There were so many good times. He was good to us financially. What was my problem? Poor Simon what he must be going through! I must be the problem. Yes he is right - I do have mental illness issues. I have always treated him so badly. So yes – looking back is not a good idea.

Friday 15th September

Mia's birthday! Mia who when she found out we were leaving said, "About f#@*ing time!" and to what address will I send a cheque? In order to get a rental property in a rental crisis and also when one does not earn the minimum wage for the rental calculator or have a rental history, one must completely rely on Jesus for a very large miracle.

Told rental agent I would pay 6 months rent up front, which was exact amount of Mia's money and Bonus from Serena paid days before rent was due. Then of course Brett's friend Gary put in a good word even though he has never met me. So here it was – a new apartment with 2 bedrooms, an attached garage, plastered, heated and insulated as a third. Comes with a fridge, washing machine, dryer, iron and ironing board. No gardening either. Just a balcony and a courtyard.

So today Rodney and I have an appointment at funeral parlour to arrange everything for Mum. I am still unpacking and going to OP Shop for stuff we do not have. Found pyjamas Mum bought me for last Christmas. How absolutely horrible. I break down sobbing. I want my Mum! Funeral is arranged for Monday 25th.

We have a lot to do before then. Photos, music, poems, clothes and then next door to pub to arrange get together after with food.

Dropped Rodney home and then had to go up to hospital again to pick up Mum's stuff. Was the worst thing possible. Drove same direction. Knew the way off by heart after going every day since she was admitted on 4th September. Parked in same spot. Mask on and into foyer. Up lift. Saw wards where she was but new different people there now. Not Mum.

Up to nurse's station. Saw palliative care room where she last was. Gone now – Gone, gone, gone!! Asked for her things. Two bags containing dressing gown and moccasins. A bag I'd bought her from our trip to UK. But by far the worst thing was the pink walking stick she took out with us on grocery day. Every Thursday, pointing and laughing. There it was with no grandma to hold it. All by itself.

OMG – Just moved in to new place, left Simon, worked this morning, gone to funeral meeting and now this. OK yes I am definitely allowed to cry. So I did. Nurse trying to comfort me. I thank her and all the staff. Then took my two bags and pink stick and sat in lounge room by myself with tears and bags and stick.

Rang Melissa (on bus). Hello – not going well – In special room with pink stick. Can't move yet. Sat a bit more. Then sucked it up. Picked up bags and stick and went down lift, back to car and home.

Monday 18th September

Still working some hours at Serena's where possible, which is the only normal thing in my life right now. Meeting celebrant at Mum's with Rodney today. Went well. Was actually quite nice reminiscing.

Tuesday 19th September

Lunchtime at work went to arrange mail re-direction. Was hysterical, panicking that Simon or mother or brother would see me. Very stupid inefficient Postal Manager organising mail re-direction with absolutely no clue!

Wednesday 20th September

Rodney and I took Mum's clothes, including rude socks, to funeral place and money to pub for Monday.

Then I am off to ballet, which I have had booked for quite some time.

Had beautiful lunch at a restaurant outside in the sun.

Pea risotto and lovely French wine.

Then ballet – so amazing, lovely, beautiful.

One week since Mum has gone.

Can't believe I am at the ballet but so glad that I am. Having the best time (including an ice-cream during intermission).

Sat 23rd September

Brett over for beers and dips / cheese.

So relaxing.

Finally allowed normal visitations.

Sunday 24th September

Beautiful sunny day.

Up early and three of us off to a regional church.

So nice – service lovely and then fish and chips on the wonderful beach.

Three of us – yes fantastic!!

Monday 25th September

Funeral Day!!

Pick up Rodney.

Haven't told Simon. No one wants him there. Up to funeral parlour. Very strange. They are lovely and so organised.

Hold Rodney's hand. I hope we will remain together regardless of all the legal stuff!

Beautiful funeral. Two songs to accommodate all of Mum's amazing photos of her life. So many lovely people.

Sunny at the pub. Such a good, amazing day. Had the best time. Then later Mel, Sam myself back for counter tea (steak). So relaxing and lovely. The most fitting end to a beautiful day!!

Friday 29th September

Simon keeps ringing. Come back. I will change. Agree to meet him because I need some stuff that I left behind, including my work uniform.

He wants me, Nick and Melissa to come back ASAP. (Not Samantha).

Saturday 30th September

Grand Final Day.

Bit weird as normally we have a big feed up.

Went grocery shopping and did lots of food. Ended up all four of us watching the game on second hand extremely large TV gifted to us by Jesus / Serena.

Thursday 5th October

11am lawyers. When finished decided to go visit Kelly (Patrick's mum) who I haven't seen for over 20 years. There was the street, there was the house and there was Kelly. All exactly the same. Like time had stood still. Big hug and inside. Everything the same inside too. Like coming home and finally feeling at peace. She is going to a church nearby, so we might come with her this Sunday. Then cafe for lunch with another old friend.

She has sent a message with a picture 'Don't Look Back – That is not the direction you are going'.

Sunday 8th October

Going to church today to meet up with Kelly. Looks like this is where we will go from now on.

Still so much to organise with lawyers for Mum's estate. Back and forth. Still arranging stuff at new place. Op shopping and buying so many bowls. Also a beautiful French cabinet that was a bargain, so yes I did need it and yes it does so fit in new place.

Ring Abigail. When spiritual warfare gets serious – you need an Abigail ASAP. Haven't spoken to Abigail for 20 years (so much has been on hold during my exile). Of course she remembers me and has been constantly praying for me all the while. We will meet up soon.

Sunday 15th October

Off to lunch at Kelly's lovely place this Sunday, after church. Just as I remember sitting at beautiful antique table with food platter that looks like it's from a fancy upmarket café.

Wednesday 19th October

Meeting with Abigail. She hasn't changed a bit. Lots of scripture and praying where two or more agree – Yes! Her car is full of goodies. Body care products for three girls. A Christmas tree – Jesus remembered years back when Patrick gifted our beautiful tree to a church family in need. I agreed but as I absolutely love Christmas, I was upset that our tree was gone. Jesus remembered and we now have the most amazing tree with built in lights. Perfect size and spectacular – of course.

Also pressies for Nick, who is a bit sceptical of all the Jesus/ church stuff (fair enough). He has been a bit annoyed that his phone stand doesn't work properly and keeps falling. Also he needs new headphones. Well Abigail gave him a phone stand, expensive headphones and some spray aftershave. "Did you tell her?" he asked.

No I didn't say anything.

"How did you know I asked my mate to buy some spray aftershave?"

I didn't.

"What are these shit headphones? Hang on," he says, "These are fantastic! These are expensive and they work so well. How come this Abigail gave all this to me?"

Well she didn't actually. It was Jesus. Even Nick had to admit it was pretty weird and strange and he even said a small thank you prayer. So there you go!

Wednesday 1st November

Going to see Simon today, as I have been summonsed. Serena and staff are awaiting my return or they will come searching for the dead body. Usual – this is all your doing and Samantha's. She is the dark cloud over our family. You have stressed out Nick and Melissa. Blah, blah, blah.

Every day I walk in the morning around the lovely lakes. I am getting to know the traffic light sequence. One particular day I was waiting for the green man. I saw the lights for the traffic go amber and then red so I stepped out onto the road and got half way across when I realised there was still a red man. Luckily no traffic as was weekend. Stopped – panicked. Was in the middle. Do I go back or keep going? Quickly ran ahead. What happened? Normally when amber, green man comes and all is safe to go.

Jesus said sometimes you assume just because usually all seems normal and has been safe, it only takes one time to change and suddenly not be safe. Be very careful of Simon. He has been fine and happy to see you each time but it only takes one meltdown to snap. OK!

Thursday 2nd November

Tree up – Yes we are allowed to now.

Simon, who by the way doesn't do Christmas on 25/12, won't allow us to put up tree early.

Friday 3rd November

Another person I haven't seen in years but have gotten in contact with is Simrin. We go for dinner. She has been through a lot also.

She knows of a woman who fled domestic violence and went back to get some clothes from amicable ex-husband and was stabbed to death. She says I have been through domestic abuse. Oh – OK!

Wednesday 8th November

NICK IS GONE! – Yes back to Simon. I said that is Ok – He is your Dad, but don't expect me to come also. There is a reason I left. I hope you realise he is abusive, nasty and has kicked us out because we are female. Anyway, I am understandably upset but not angry.

Woke up in the morning after learning of this last night. Jesus was saying, *"lean not on your own understanding"*. OK – will try to do that. Wonder how housework will go.

Naughty Abigail would love to be a fly on the wall. I am very, very upset that Nick has gone. However, Jesus has asked, *"who is your God? Me or your children?"* OK – I have to let them go because Jesus / God is the most important thing to me. Also he has reminded me about Abraham / Isaac and the sacrifice. So OK

I will be upset about Nick but I will give him and our relationship to you Jesus. So here we go again – More grieving. First Mum, then Simon and now Nick. Seriously, do I have any tears left? So awful, so, so, so awful to continuously feel like this! I would love to feel happiness for just 5 minutes!

I have realised that I have never had any affection from someone in a relationship. Simon hated affection. He only wanted sex and only when he wanted it. Not me. When he wanted it, I had to be available also regardless of how I felt. If I tried to show him some affection by hugging him or trying to give him a quick kiss, he would say, "Oh God, you're all over me. Right-O let me have some space and we'll do it later". Which of course never happened unless he wanted sex. Which was, "let's get this over and done with."

Patrick on the other hand hated sex with a female. We did it once or twice because he felt an obligation as we were married. I was left to feel unattractive and lonely within a marriage. It was awful. He regularly had affairs with guys. I knew as I could feel it. He also admitted to some and would then apologise profusely and promise never to do it again. Through the church he did conversion therapy. Personally I think gay people can be Christians who love Jesus. It might not be the ideal biblical way but no one is without sin and is living in the ideal biblical way on earth. If pretending not to be gay hurts others, then that is harmful and unfair. So let them be gay and not involve and hurt unsuspecting Christians who have done nothing to deserve this. Let them sort this out themselves with God and Jesus!

I now own Mum's car. Not sure what I will do with it, but anyway! Went to Rodney to give him money and get keys. He is like a small child, having many tantrums about Mum's estate. Currently I have so much shit being hurled at me, I don't need any extra so I am ready for a fight. Instead I pray and loudly at that. I pray that the strongman will be bound in our relationship and this transaction and that any demons or satanic attacks will be rendered useless and unable to cause any damage until I have left the building. In their place Holy Spirit and angels are to come and bring restoration and peace. So I get there and Rodney is all lovely, signing forms, apologising and telling me all is going to be OK. Don't stress! So we go through some more of Mum's stuff. I get the car keys and Rodney gives me a big hug and tells me he loves me.

You may be wondering why I would stay with Simon for 20 years. I had to. To protect the children. If I left he would have had half custody. One week on / one week off. That would mean they would have also been taken to the grandparents and possibly whisked away to their country. I was supposed to hand them over to her and then work full time. The grandparents got quite abusive and threatening so the police advised me to get a restraining order against them. I had to go to the court by myself, pregnant with Melissa. She had a team of lawyers, who when they found out the real reason they were there, came to me and asked if I needed anything and was I OK? Simon knew all this and basically blamed me and said "You always attract drama – Don't you". He and his mother said none of it was true and I had made up stories to get them in trouble. So the death threats continued and I slept with a golf club under my bed, when I could sleep.

So I stayed with the children 24/7 for 20 years so that they were never left alone with Simon and his family. I was harassed over the phone. I was followed. My mum was followed. I lived in constant fear that she would take the children. She turned up to the Kinder in a disguise to speak to the children. It was terrifying. All the while Simon blamed me for causing dramas with his family. He still saw them and would come back telling me how much they hated me.

One day at the shopping centre I could physically feel that I was being followed. It was the strangest feeling. I kept looking behind me. I had the kids with me. The next day Simon said, "my Mum saw you. You weren't comforting Nick when he was crying at the shops. You are a bad mother." If I was then I realised my weird feeling was justified. Initially when I first had the children

I was commanded by Simon to take them to his mother every other day. It was exhausting. She would grab them and feed them and ignore me. Then she would complain to Simon that I hadn't given her enough time with them. So he would demand that I go around to her house and apologise. I was constantly told I was a bad mother and she should take over.

I was a bad mother and also a woman, so my opinion did not count.

Sunday 12th November

How lovely – Nick has sent Melissa a happy snap of a restaurant table filled with expensive food including a huge steak feast. Yes, Simon has taken him out and then sent a cruel photo to us to show off. "You should have come" was the message.

Melissa and Samantha were going to send explosive SMS's back but I told them not to. Just say, "Oh that looks nice. Maybe next time." I don't have it in me to be nasty and vindictive. Would have been like me sending a photo of us enjoying food together on Grand Final Day, which is our big family feast normally. I wouldn't even think of doing that to him for a second, as I know it would be very hurtful. Oh well that's the difference between us right there, isn't it.

Message at church was you are not here by accident today. Forget the past and forge forward. Forget is not remembering by not thinking about it. Forging is hard work but comes out beautiful.

Sunday 26th November

Have hang over – 80's Festival last night. Amanda and Jemma over. Kelly lunch. Simon rang, not to wish Happy Birthday but to demand I come back. Nick is so much happier now that he is back. He was miserable with me. It was unbearable. I haven't tried to ring him. Yes I have. He didn't answer. He wants us to be a family unit. Melissa would rather be miserable with me than happy with Simon because she will always want to be where I am. Simon says I have been rude and stand offish to him for the last few years but he was happy to suffer through it! Delusional!! I tried so hard to please him. However apparently not good enough.

Nick just rang. He wants it to be how it was before with us as a family unit (without Samantha of course). He is so much happier now back with Simon. Simon will be so much nicer now, he is sure of it. He did not say being here was unbearable. He will only come to Christmas if Simon can come too! Wow!!! Did not once say Happy Birthday.

In Simon's culture, first born is the most important child. So Samantha and Simon were to be worshipped by all other siblings and waited on by their mothers. I guess that is why he decided Sam was dead to him now. She had to be, otherwise firstborn rule would still apply. Nick is number one now.

Thursday 30th November

Ah!!

So much going on at work right now. I just love it all so much. Stress doesn't really explain it correctly. I am being manipulated and made to feel guilty by all parties. I am going to move on. However Serena is doomed and having a tantrum. I have been there for so long. However, I believe everything is becoming new in my life now. This is the most eye opening thing for me so far.

Friday 1st December

Off to new job today. A bit uppity and demanding. New boss is a 'no-show.' Not really feeling the vibe. So will stay at Serena/new owner. Really don't need the extra stress thank you so much.

Sunday 3rd December

Didn't go to weekend trip. Only go if you have a boat. Very flooded. You know it's not a good idea when the lady from the accommodation is saying maybe best not to come. It might be unsafe. So went to church. Reject, resist, replace. Thank you Jesus again. Doorbell – Who should be there? Nick plus one – one being Simon. I know right.
Seriously. In the words of Abigail, "Not a good idea mate."

Wanted to come in. I told that narcissistic demon, "Ah – that's a straight no." Looked very pleased with itself – did that spirit of control and manipulation. Can't say the same for Nick, who had his head down most of the time.

"How did you get a rental in a rental crisis?" I told him that would be Jesus. Anyway Jemma had gone to get Melissa from work and came over once they left. They were both stressed and upset. I told them to sit and have some pâté and cheese. After something awful going on everyday, this is just normal for me, so really not that fussed.

Tuesday 5th December

Nick no longer talking to me. Must have blocked my number. Oh well upsetting, but nothing I can do at this stage, except pray.

Thursday 7th December

Oh Nick has decided to grace us with his presence. Especially when there is mention of his car in my name and will be taken if he doesn't transfer into his before Roadworthy expires.

He says that he probably won't speak to me anymore as most likely I won't be coming back home with Dad. Upsetting but I am not going to be manipulated by the arrogant, defiant, uncaring demon that has taken up residence in Nick. Sorry – Not Sorry!!!!

Saturday 10th December

Went back to Simon's house. Put on full armour of God and prayed for angels, especially big one in 'camo-gear'. Went into demonic pit. Could see the occasional demon in Simon's face. Also Nick's. Apparently I have caused much upset and trauma to all. I am in a cult. I have a mental illness but Simon will put up with all that as he usually has to, if I will come back.

"Yes Mum, you need to come back to have a happy family but DO NOT bring Samantha. She is a dark cloud over all of us!"

Let's have a look in the mirror – shall we?

Got out of there as quick as I could with some bits and pieces. Couldn't bring too much, as Simon believes I will be back soon and I didn't want a large altercation about that.

Monday 11th December

Through a friend of a friend, I have found out information about Nick. He is going through a very horrible time. Melissa and Samantha both happy stating "Karma".

I am crying because he is still my boy. He must be very upset and panicking about money. He obviously feels it would be better for him to go back to live with Dad. Dad will pay for everything he wants, including WIFI. So he has blatantly lied to my face about this. Not sure why. Maybe embarrassed. I don't know. Sent him a text saying I love him so much. Heard nothing back. Oh well.

Thursday 14th December

My life is so full on. Do I wish it was boring? Yes, but mostly – No, actually.

So much going on:

New Job
New Holidays
New House
New/old friends

I feel like Job – lost everything but am gaining back so much.

Friday 15th December

Well I have booked Europe for Jan 10. Feel very bad and guilty. Everyone will be let down. Shouldn't go. Then I see a website about self-worth. Apparently I don't have that. Never have. When I was little, Dad always told me I wasn't good enough. Then Patrick, then Simon. So I believed them. Anyway, I have prayed regarding upcoming trip / trips, job / jobs, money outings, etc.

Up at 3.30am again. There is a website message on my phone. Really? I just want to sleep! Will have a very quick look.

> *"God has spoken to you. Receive those things that were taken away from you. Be happy and be glad. Like Job (yes that is me) everything that was taken away from him was restored back in multiplied fold. This is about to happen to you now. That honour that you deserve. No more lack.*

Troubles are taken away from you now. God is doing new things in your life. Do you believe in these words that God is saying to you? Have you accepted that God is going to change your life very soon? Are you seeing yourself in that new life now? Those things that you have lost are coming back to you. Not just the way they left you but in a better way that will make your life amazing to tell others."

OK – Well talk about seeing the writing on the wall (slash phone). Right, so this is the day that the Lord has made. I will rejoice and be glad in it!! I will enjoy my interstate trip. Then beautiful countryside, then fireworks for New Year. Then Europe and London. I am trying to believe that yes – I do deserve all this and new job too.

Going to church Christmas tonight for carols.

Wow – I realise I only believe I deserve bad stuff, not good.

Tuesday 19th December

Off to interstate holiday.

Blessings:

Credit for Melissa's ticket. Upgraded both ways on flights.

3 hour earlier flight home on the way back so not late to Kelly's Christmas Eve dinner. Dorothy giving me a lift to Island tour. Only person dropped off by bus back to Villa after Island tour. Amazing French Villa on the waterfront. French provincial furnishings everywhere. Complimentary champagne and wine. Beautiful grounds. Old fashioned Christmas music tinkling away. A sparkly Christmas tree.

Haven't seen a single soul other than different servant girls to tend to me. I feel like a princess being waited on. I walk down the stairs and a maid appears and sits me in the drawing room with a drink and then takes me through to the dining room all by myself, where I am cooked a steak and served alone, cleaned up after and fussed over. I am surrounded by all of my favourite things. I don't deserve this. I have a panic attack. I must be dead! This is heaven. Must have died on the way over. Had a plane crash or died in the taxi trip down. Car crash and I didn't know and just woke up here. I am not ready to die yet. Also where is Jesus if I am in Heaven? Samantha rings. She is unwell. I ask her if I am dead. No Mum! Oh my goodness!

Anyway last girl has now gone for the night. So I am here all by myself now in a giant chateau / villa / castle. Three levels. I now have to go everywhere. Library, sitting room, dining room, drawing room, parlour, etc. and pray angels / Holy Spirit in and demons out. Sorry Jesus, bit of a big job for you here. Rang Abigail and Kelly for extra prayer cover. Yes Jesus is Lord! How weird my life is – but also good thanks.

Whilst on this time out holiday I have had to sit and have been forced to relax. I have been told: "Nick did not leave, he was removed! Oh – OK then!!

It is so quiet here. I am in my room like a Covid lockdown looking out to the water and chateau grounds. God says, *"Be still and know that I AM GOD!!"* Oh – OK!!

Abigail says to check with God first but it could be an idea to pray and curse any friendships Nick has that are not OK. When Jesus cursed the fig tree it happened within 24 hours, so be careful. Simrin rang. She believes it is crucial to help Nick ASAP, as she knows the signs of drug abuse and mental illness.

OK I have a sign. So I pray at an outdoor fountain to curse any friendships Nick has that need to wither. Will see what develops.

Saturday 23rd December

Island tour.

The lovely Dorothy picks me up on her day off and waits with me for my bus. Have the best day. Must buy her something at the chocolate place. Searching, searching. Find a lovely little tin with chocolates in it. Yes that's it! Give it to her next morning. She can't believe it. This is her ultimate favourite thing. She collects these. How did I know? Not even from the Island – is from UK.

Well thank you Jesus. He always knows the best presents for people. Who would have thought?

Sunday 24th December

Leaving today. Flight at 3.45. Arriving 5.15. Supposed to be at Kelly's by 6. I don't think so. Anyway Jesus says get organised. I am putting you on an earlier flight.

Oh no Jesus I don't think so. It will be very busy being Christmas Eve. Also my taxi isn't booked until 12pm. Probably will be a fee to change it.

Jesus says, *"You are getting an earlier flight so ring the taxi and see if they can pick you up sooner. Do not do online check in."* But I always do online check in as soon as it opens!!!

So consequently taxi got there early. Got an earlier flight (3 hours) with no fees. Thank you Jesus.

Monday 25th December

Jesus' Birthday.

I wake up early. I am exhausted from trip and Kelly's. I am not getting up yet and definitely not going to church this morning. Having Rodney over for Christmas lunch. <u>Nothing</u>, I mean <u>nothing</u> is done, as I have been away. I need to sleep as we have Abigail's also for tonight's Christmas. Jesus says get up now. I will help you with the lunch and you will not feel tired all day. So I got up and everything got done and I felt so rested and awake. Look at that. Time to get dressed and arrive at church on time. Thank you Jesus.

Pray over apartment and front door. Anoint with oil and Melissa and I pray wherever two or more are gathered and agree that any demons must stay away or stay subdued and quiet.

Rodney arrives. Goes very well. He has a great time.

Wednesday 27th December

My wine glasses have arrived. A present from Samantha, as she knows how much I love them. Very hard to find, but she has. They made my heart sing a million songs and my eyes cry a million tears!!

That's all. Good night!!

Monday 1st January 2024

HAPPY NEW YEAR!!!

God has just told me to get this book and write down:

See I am doing a new thing. Do you not perceive it?? I am making streams in the wasteland.

I have just been lying on the floor unable to move. Melissa has been watching me and crying. I said I do not want to go on. I can't go on. I wish I was dead!!!

Everything feels as though it is going wrong. Serena, Rodney, sale of house or rather *no sale*. Mum dead. Cemetery Plaque. Nick ignoring and blocking. Simon demanding me to come back. Also now I have just had an epiphany. I have to gain consent from Simon to travel with Melissa. So can't go – cancel everything. Lose all the money. What was I thinking, going on a trip? Must not have been God's plan or will.

God has shown me he is in control. Trust in me. You are going – Go get your book and write **that** down – right now!! See I am doing a new thing. You must rely on me. Do not be anxious about anything but with prayer and petition present your requests to God. Rely on me. He showed me photos from interstate trip when I thought I died and went to heaven. He showed me Dorothy's present. Be still and know that I am God!!

He showed me stuff on my phone explaining that Satan is attacking me. Do not accept that. Pray to me – Jesus. Jesus is my Lord and Saviour. That's all!!

Actually no that's not all – Got up and walked out into apartment hall. Jesus says, "*Where are you?? Look at this apartment – Where did this come from? Remember I can do all things through Him who gives me strength. Write that down also.*"

Oh Boy – Been told to write more in the book. During my latest trip I felt that I didn't deserve good things. Can't be true. Must be dead and in heaven. No Jesus says, you do deserve it and He has just reminded me of this and says that is what a European holiday is. It is a good gift given by your Father in heaven. Ok – so is that all I need to write in this jolly book for now? We shall see.

Jesus has shown me that Satan is attacking me to stop me from being a person of God. He has been trying to shut me up (even kill me) for the longest time.

Tuesday 2nd January

Got in contact with lawyers who are doing Mum's estate regarding taking a child out of the country. All good to go as long as no court orders or proceedings. So good off we go!!

Friday 5th January

Yay!! Happy Birthday Nick!! Always go bowling. Going bowling as usual, without Nick this time and also without grandma. That's ok because we have Amanda and Kelly instead. I win – Of course!! Yay!!

Still not convinced regarding travel consent from Simon. OK – Will print out travel consent and see if Simon will sign. Yes because on Wednesday printer miraculously came to life after being dead since we moved here. Without WIFI. Apparently using WIFI direct. Not sure what that is but Jesus does. Maybe Bluetooth or something. I don't know!! All I know is dormant printer is now working to printout travel consent.

Then Simon rings. He is screaming so loud that Melissa can hear him upstairs without being on speaker from downstairs bedroom with door closed. But no – he is not yelling, he is just very frustrated with me!! I am very selfish and apparently I am in a cult and I am sleeping with so many men. Ok not sure who they are but if you say so!! Wants me and Melissa to come tomorrow at 12pm to discuss coming back.

Yeah sure!! Will I bring all of my boyfriends? Anyway we will go with printed travel consent to sign also. Praying to Jesus. Let your will be done with all of this. Seriously!!

Saturday January 6th

Website – Parents, never stop praying over your children. If they want to go (be detached) and pursue their own dreams, let them. No matter what things may look like. Pray without ceasing. Speak life over them. God's will shall be done in their life. Then one day your prayers will be answered. Keep your faith. Also another guy on Website in movie industry, was offered a 'deal' from Satan. Did not take it. However God showed him another movie star that did and he is so successful now. At what cost?

Anyway Simon signed the form. I prayed that if we were not supposed to go then he wouldn't. So looks like all good to go.

Thursday 11th January

Arrive Munich (in thick fog)

Slightly terrifying!! However, we touch down (runway unseen). Jesus says that's how you are to believe with blind faith. Spoke to Brett. Apparently in Europe they have technology that talks to each other to bring the plane in without the pilot seeing anything. That's how it is being a Christian.

Jesus very busy with us:

- New boots for Melissa worth $500 but only paid $70;
- Get into room 5 hours early to sleep;
- Shows me website for driver to get us from Prague to Dresden;
- Shows me bus to Brussels / Bruges instead of three trains.
- Lots of Websites – including removing objects from your home. Jewellery, crystals, books, etc;
- Lots to throw out when we get back.

Friday 26th January

Website – lady says – not sure who needs to hear this but your children are being used to manipulate against you. I pray against this for you in the mighty name of Jesus. Wasn't even searching this up. Anyway I will accept this. Amen!!

Saturday 27th January

Well what can I say? Concert tonight! On me, oh my!! Poor angels that I prayed to come with. So exciting to go. So packed. So amazing. But oh so, so evil, bad, satanic, demonic. They have taken 'The Deal'.

Oh Boy!!! We had to sit there in the midst of actual hell on earth with our angels, who must have been quite annoyed I would think. It was awful and scary.

Finally got out after commanding two demons to let us pass and after much anger and abuse they had to. Well you live and learn or at least we hope so and our angels hope so.

Wednesday 31st January

Back. Yay!! Not.

Friday 8th March 2024

Last night snakes dream: Someone throwing it at me. Hissing and fangs coming at me. Message at lunch from random guy on website. "This is not a coincidence that you are hearing this message. People are about to get back in contact with you because you have an inheritance coming. Be aware and do not be scammed by them. This is a warning!!"

Then tonight out of the blue – Haven't heard from Nick in months, since a message whilst we were in Europe being extremely abusive about me coming back to Simon. Just wondering if we can meet up one day. I say of course but weird I got this message today. Then immediately went to website and of course Lindy has a message. Snakes!! Be careful of them. They will hide until they want to be noticed. They will shed their skin only to get progressively bigger. They will attack you when you least expect it. You may be expecting them to bite but not always. Sometimes they will strangle you and you will not be able to breathe. When you can't breathe you will know there is a snake attacking you.

Not sure what is going down with Nick and Simon but Jesus does. We will wait and see!!! Fiddledee Dee!!

Do not take the bait says Lindy again.

Friday 29th March (Good Friday)

Coming out of Egypt. Preparing a table in the presence of my enemies. God is preparing a new season for you. Your enemies will be shocked!

Monday 8th April

Mum's car is going to be towed. Have to join RACV and leave work early. Give car to a friend. He has to get RWC and then transfer out of my name. Nightmares!!

Tuesday 16th April

Oh My Goodness. Apparently I have just bought a house!!! OK – Thank you Jesus.

Saw house on Saturday 8th April with Melissa. First one. So, so many more to see. Thank you very much. Then last Saturday 13th April was busy looking at others. Ran in last five minutes of inspection. Yes, very nice!!

Then God sent me for a walk up the road and there I was with a statue overlooking the Promised Land. (The beach where I have always wanted to be). I cried. I couldn't believe it. Overwhelmed. Amazing. Have been praying regarding a house. Then today I rang real estate agent. All of a sudden I put in an offer. Vendor said no! "OK," I said, "that's fine. I will live overseas then." Yep –

started googling houses. Yep that's where I am going!! Then 10pm message. He will accept your next offer.

OK here comes the skipping that Lindy was talking about. Can you believe I am actually buying a house by the beach? Thank you Jesus. Better do so very full on fasting this Thursday.

Wednesday 17th April 2024

Signed contract for house.

Thursday 18th April 2024

Fasting for Auction. Fasting is not about food. Tithing is not about money.

Final meeting with real estate agent. Paid first deposit for house.

Video came up all by itself – I am putting you into your home. God is establishing order into your life. It won't be long now. There will be an overflowing and you will be placed into your home.

Friday 19th April 2024

Building and Pest inspection 9am. Rings me – All bad news. Roof is horrific. Very rusted. Wouldn't buy it. Abort, abort abort!!!!

Panic stations. Ring Real Estate agent. Cool off now. Lawyer /Conveyancer to draft cooling off letter to send to other conveyancer. Ring Luke BANK – cancel. Sorry Jesus you have it all wrong – we have to cancel now. Had big hissy fit in car on the way home. Yelled at Jesus – Why me? Why, why, why? So much stuff – Dad. Patrick. Simon. Nick. Serena. Mum dying. Hormone headaches for 15 years. New job. No money. Mum's car. Now this – lost house. I can no longer go on. I can't. I want to be dead. Please kill me now and I meant it.

Be aware the first instant that you have a moment of weakness, the enemy will pounce. Whoosh and he is there!!

Then I felt someone saying – Yes this world is very hard if you rely on Jesus. You have seen the success and money that can be yours here on earth. You have seen musicians and others that are thriving. How easy it will be for you on earth if you come with me. Don't worry about later when you eventually die. Enjoy now like they are. How amazing your life will be. Everything can be yours. It will be so long in the future when you die. Don't even think about it. It is so far off. I know it would be easier here on earth for sure. I have seen it. However, I know this life is so much more than just here on earth. Then I felt it say "OK – well the other way to avoid all the pain and sorrow you are going through is to commit suicide. Then it will all go away and you will finally have peace. So much easier.

I was in the midst of total helplessness and so much grief. I was overwhelmed by everything that has happened to me. I was unable to go on. Wow – As soon as a tiny crack appears – BOOM – There is Satan with his temptation. Yes it would be easier. However, I am a child of God and although it is hard and exhausting I could never not follow Jesus Christ my amazing father. Even if I am mad at him right now. It's like a family member you are pissed at in the moment. You will get over it and move on. I am so sorry Jesus. I have apologised and asked for so much forgiveness and am meekly holding onto his hand for today.

Saturday 20th April 2024

Auction Day. Jesus will be there. Whatever he wants will happen. Rusty roof is having an inspection today. Jesus's will shall be done in my life. Jesus has a home (not house) for me somewhere. I believe and I receive.

Feeling very down and weak after yesterday's debarkle. What to wear for an Auction? Go upstairs says Jesus and open clothes trunk. Pull out tunic thing. Yes looks Auction approved. Get dressed, do hair and make-up. All in black head to foot except large red stripe going around chest. Yes red. Mums favourite colour that we were to wear at funeral. Wore a red top that day. Don't ever wear red. Anyway was told to write that in book – so here it is. Write this down also – A tree waits in the acorn. A bird waits in the egg. Dreams will come to be.

Auction – Goes well. Kelly there. Abigail there. Jesus there.

Jesus has told me I am set free from parental home. Didn't think childhood home was a bad place but it was and it is going to be gone from my life and I am moving on.

Sunday 21st April

Feel all wrong about house. I know that unit was mine from Jesus. Sorry Jesus. I would actually like it back thank you.

OK he says, so you better ring everybody back hadn't you and buy it again. So I did. Luke from BANK answered his phone on Sunday. Also Real Estate agent.

Monday 22nd April

I have my beautiful beach house back. I know, I know. Rusty roof and all!! Auction went well. Not huge but enough to pay for old rusty. Owner was prepared to take money off to compensate for possible roof restoration in the future. So paid lower price and longer settlement to coincide with Mum's.

Back down to bank to pay big deposit. I enter the bank and boom!! All computers and ATM's down. Everybody has to leave the bank except for me as I am at the teller already. Girl has to put through manually. Takes around 2 hours. Eventually done. Seriously Satan!!!

Then I had to sign loan documents on line. Of .course they are experiencing system issues. Try again later. Rang BANK – Rang Luke. They don't know what is going on. All home loans are down. Down since 1pm. Tried until 9pm. Nothing. Eventually managed to sign but couldn't input other info but mostly all done.

God says, *"Well done my good and faithful servant. You have done all you can do. I will take it from here!"*

Tuesday 23rd April

SOLD!!

Contract all signed. Jesus is King.

This time last year I was going to live in my car.

Thursday 25th April

Sold sticker on board. With an ANZAC Day march to celebrate down our street.

Of course.

My photo is in the local newspaper (very small but still in).

July 2024

Mum's settlement is about to happen. Panic stations, as I have no idea if there will be enough funds to cover the settlement of my new house. Including stamp duty and fees. I ring the conveyancer. She doesn't know the exact amount required but it is very tight. I ask her what will happen if there is not enough money. Well it will be a legal nightmare apparently. Great! Oh well, help Jesus. Of course he does. After all the calculations, there is just enough to cover everything.

Reading all this and living through it really is an amazing, huge miracle and blessing from God. This stuff would not happen 'IRL', which I am told is 'In Real Life' for SMS purposes!!!!!

January 2025

Went away.

I have come to write this book. All going well.

Came home.

Sick, so very, very sick.

February 2025

Sick does not really explain how I feel. I would love to kill myself. However, I can't as I will go to Hell.

Although, currently I am in a worse place than Hell.

The only way I have gotten through this is with Jesus. I have not "walked through the Valley of the shadow of death". I have been dragged through "the Valley of actual death" by my hair.

Three months of sheer hell. No book writing. No catching up with friends. No eating. No exercise. Pain, pain and no sleep. Demons, witchcraft, sorcery, black magic, hell. I have prayed and fasted. Jesus has been with me. It has been horrible. He is the only reason I am still here.

May 2025

Away to a weekend retreat. Finishing book.

Still so very sick. Jesus heals. I believe that.

June 2025

Book finally being organised.

No weapon formed against me shall prosper!

Being Healed.

Feeling better.

Thank you Jesus.

www.ingramcontent.com/pod-product-compliance
Lightning Source LLC
LaVergne TN
LVHW050935080826
845145LV00004B/1274

* 9 7 8 1 7 6 4 1 3 6 2 3 5 *